The Clam Hunter

The Clam Hunter

David Marshall

To order additional copies of this book, contact:
Xlibris Corporation
1-888-795-4274
www.Xlibris.com
Orders@Xlibris.com
73619

Contents

Dedication

This book was written in memory of Jim
and is dedicated to my daughter Sarah.

THE CLAM HUNTER

Since the beginning of the human existence, recorded in the form of crude animal renderings drawn on cave walls, it would appear that hunting was fundamental, primordial part of man. Built into our genetic framework and passed on for eons, the instinct to hunt at the very least contributed to our survival. Some would argue that without this component human evolution would never have taken place. Chronologically, the amount of time that has passed since assuming our present-day, sedentary role of farmer is slight when compared to our much longer history as that of hunter-gatherer. All animals hunt for food. Even a clam itself will hunt for microscopic algae by deliberately positioning its body into the lower layers of the water column. Discordant is the idea that hunting is always a savage act involving bloodshed. In its strictest sense, hunting is simply the act of pursuing something. Perhaps anything. We hunt for food, mates, happiness, spiritual states of being, peace. Some of us will even employ passion, determination, and eventual understanding to find and collect but a single animal faintly calling out in the tidal marsh, We are here! We are here!

A Note from the Author

I never intended to spend as much time in search of the clam as I ended up doing. Entire years were consumed. I was consumed, perhaps not so much with a physical resource but rather with an idea. The clam simply became a representation of everything I deem as wild, natural and pure in this world. The clam in my eyes became an ambassador to the isolated and yet disappearing world of the tidal salt marsh. According to best guess estimates we have lost over half of the wetlands in the U.S. since the arrival of European colonists. They have been drained, paved over, and filled in to better accommodate the developer and farmer. We are finally beginning to understand the significance of these areas both from a biological perspective as well as from a more esoteric view point. You cannot put a price tag on the visions that nature affords. Once these places are gone they are gone for good. Hopefully it is not too late to save that which remains. In a metaphorical sense, it simply takes the planting of a single seed to establish an entire forest. I would like to think that this seed is represented by the basic ideas presented in this book. This seed will lie dormant until these ideas are examined and acted upon. Meanwhile, the clam will hold on steadfast, burrowed under, trying to support and improve a place that has by most gone unappreciated and ignored.

PROLOGUE

JULY 15, 2001

The sweet smell of salt grass filled the air and seemed to usher in what promised to be another sultry day on the Eastern Shore. A week in the doldrums of summer. According to the unmoving grass in the tidal marsh the stillness would prevail. The quiet desolation of this place always appeared surreal in contrast to the frantic world of the mainland that only a few hours ago he had left behind. He was working in an area just west of Parramore Island. For a change, the day had been profitable, and he was returning in good spirits back to the boat with a large bag filled with small clams. Considering the small, higher-priced clams, the value of this single bag approximated one hundred dollars. Good money for a clammer. He was in a particular hurry this day to get back to the dock. Stores were closing and he needed to buy a part to fix his truck. He decided to take a short-cut through the marsh. Though the walk back to the boat was cut in half, the journey first required getting across a very deep, albeit narrow channel. After a few minutes of deliberation he decided to lunge his body forward while holding onto the bag of clams. He assumed that by doing so he would have enough momentum to grab hold of the opposite bank. He assumed wrong. He watched in horror as the entire days profits disappeared into the abysmal deep. This particular channel, being cut out by abnormally strong currents had a depth ranging anywhere from 12-15 feet in its middle. After mumbling several curse words, he got out of the water, stripped off his clothes, took a deep breath and dove back in. As the water was too murky to see anything, he found the bag only by probing the silty bottom with his hands. He took hold of the top of the bag with both hands and slowly walked it up the other side by jamming his feet into the steep and muddy embankment. By the time his head broke the surface of the water, somewhere between two to three minutes had elapsed. No one was around. What help would they have been if they were. A lot of energy had been expended to get these clams only to lose them this way. He got the bag onto solid ground at the edge of the channel and sat down on top of it. After saying a prayer of thanks to our Lord and redressing himself he continued back to the boat.

For the few people who clam here, it was just another day in the marsh. And like the proverbial tree in the forest, if I were not writing about it now, no one would even know that it ever happened.

Map Showing a section of the Eastern Shore of Virginia
Scale 1: 80,000
(Courtesy of Washington D.C. Dept. of Commerce NOAA National Ocean Coast Survey North American Datum of 1983 World Geodetic System of 1984)

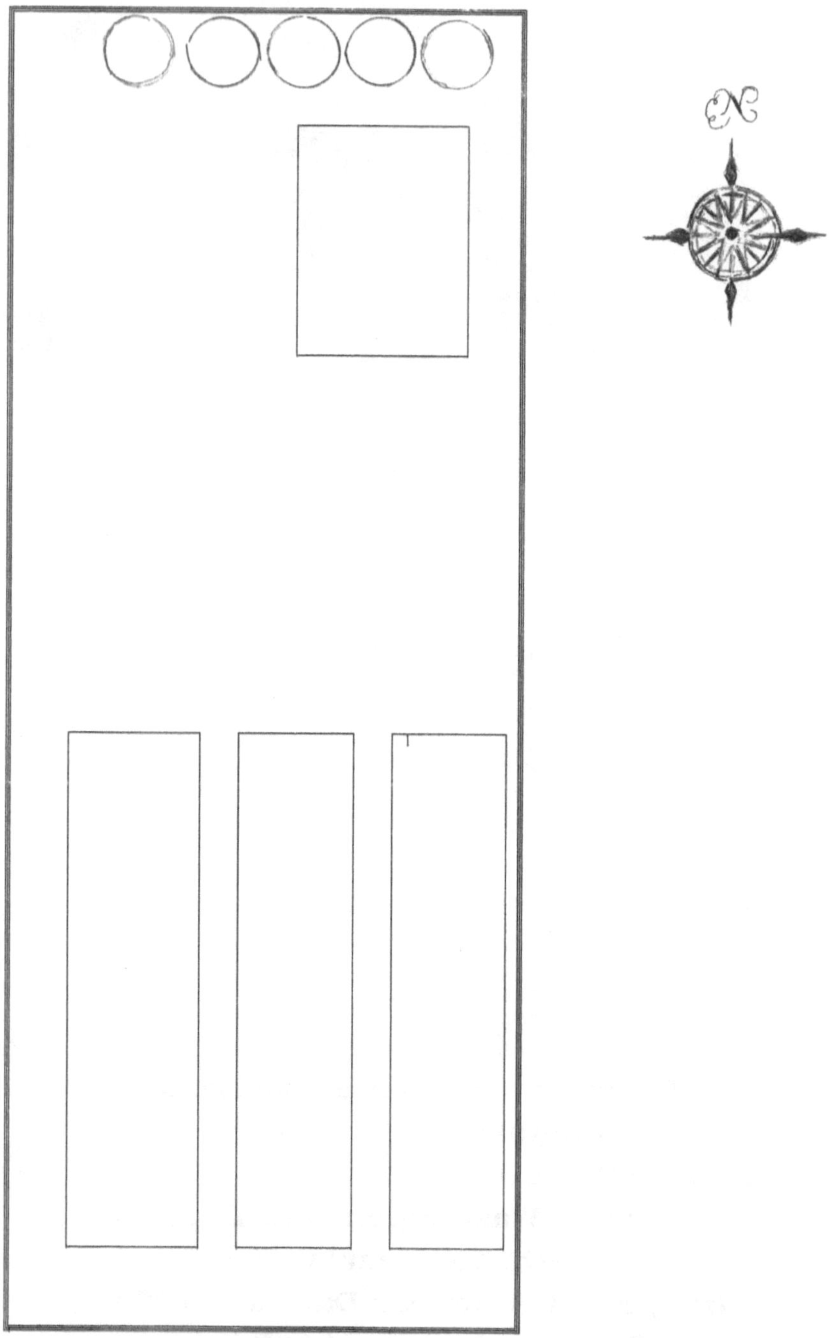

Clam hatchery layout and design

ACKNOWLEDGEMENTS

To a group of commercial fisherman living and working on the Eastern Shore:

I wish to thank: Joe Boulter, Ed Lee Stratton, Greg Stratton, Mark Camm, Anjelo, and. Junior

I also wish to express my thanks to Jackie Paul Dwyer for editing this book. Her support and devotion has made life better.

Cover photograph: Courtesy of Donna Sharp (2007)

CHAPTER I

THE FORMIDABLE YEARS

He was a "come here". A reclusive individual with an independent spirit who, with his dog Jim, showed up one morning on the seaside of the Eastern Shore to venture into places unknown. He was trying to find clams and more importantly trying to establish a new lifestyle.

At first glance the locals simply saw a stranger who apparently liked going out on the water. Probably a sightseer or just an ardent fisherman. He seemed to be consistent enough showing up almost every day with boat in tow, hustling at the dock, trying to get underway. And always leaving during that part of the day when the tides were falling.

Other watermen caught on quickly as to what he was doing, but the general public for the most part hadn't a clue. Rumors spread quickly and before long this rogue fisherman was either running drugs, using the clams as cover, or was stealing clams planted under nets or from privately leased ground. Though none of this was true, the stranger seemed to be in no hurry to reveal his specific intentions. In fact, some years passed before many locals realized exactly what he was doing. It is not in a fisherman's best interest to volunteer information as to how and where something is caught. Word gets around and before you know it the resource has been depleted or the market has become depressed. Besides, if someone truly wants to find something they have to look for it themselves.

He was from another place at another time. Before setting foot on the Shore he hardly knew what a clam was. Former occupations included that of carpenter, landscaper, retail clerk, teacher, environmentalist, cross country ski instructor, park ranger, lab technician, and truck driver. His name was Maxwell. His quiet demeanor along with the degree of conviction to which he worked both seemed to add elements of mystery to his character. And like the clam he would not, perhaps could not, be easily understood. Even the law seemed to be at odds with this man. Though he would not run from either the VMRC or Coast Guard he seemed to be constantly trying to avoid them. Almost expending as much energy in trying to become invisible to the law as he was trying to become invisible to the clam. He would spend entire days slipping quietly in and out of guts (small channels adjoining larger bodies of water), searching for clams and also avoiding the lengthy delays of boat searches and safety checks from law enforcement personnel. Most of these guts are too shallow for boats to navigate in. As well near a guts head (place where a gut starts) a person, even standing up, cannot be seen. In general there is an eight foot variation between a high and a low tide on the Eastern Shore. Such considerable variation creates high banks in a gut on a low tide making them ideal to hide in. They also contain huge numbers of clams that can only be reached on the lowest of tides. Given these factors, Maxwell could spend a considerable part of the day working in isolation undetected by anyone who happened to pass by. However, there always seemed to be problems either going out or coming back in. He was constantly scrutinized. His attempt at secrecy seemed to work well in catching the elusive clam and yet failed miserably in avoiding the law. Perhaps he looked as if he were doing something wrong.

On more than one occasion he was reprimanded and fined for running a boat at night without lights. Light can be a distraction and having it near ones face while trying to navigate a boat in shallow water at night can be a major problem. Ones vision becomes more acute (pupil size changing) without light interference. Once adjusted to the dark, the eyes are capable of discerning subtle changes in hues thus indicating the depth of the water. One is also better able to see silhouettes. A silhouette from say a tree or tall marsh grass can be all that you have to distinguish between land and water. Such information becomes critical to anyone running a boat at night outside of main channels between the mainland and Barrier Islands on the Eastern Shore. Though people might not be able to see you, you can see them, and your chance of avoidance without running aground is greatly increased. Granted this line of reasoning would not hold up in heavy boat traffic or in areas where large ships need to see things well in advance to make any corrections in direction. Unfortunately the laws are not always specific enough to take everything into account.

In any case, whatever money was made from the discovery of new, untapped caches of clams, always seemed to be offset by heavy fines imposed by state enforcement officials. Sometimes warranted and sometimes not. It was not as if he was trying to buck the system. He was not always aware of the many rules and regulations governing the harvest of clams, even by hand, but he was not deliberately trying to break any laws.

I have heard it said, the commercial fisherman is slowly being regulated right out of business. Like any other commercial fisherman, Maxwell was trying to feed people, and at times with considerable sacrifice. As well, he was trying to harvest a sustainable resource. Who better to take care of a resource than one who relies on it as a source of income. Great measure would be taken to leave an ample number of clams (all sizes), such that they could repopulate themselves. In fact, Maxwell would go back to many areas that he had worked before only to find clams in even greater numbers. By opening up the bottom substrate, or breaking it apart, in essence, can give veliger larvae (early growth clams) a more suitable place to burrow in. This will be explained later in further detail. Suffice it to say, Maxwell's early years on the water were fraught with resistance. Some of this resistance simply coming from mother nature, most of it coming from people. As I guess with any place harboring small town communities, people on the Shore make it their business to know your business. Especially when the person in question is not from their area. Whether factual or fictitious, word spreads like wildfire and before you know it your character is branded. People generally believe what is the easiest and/or the most convenient to comprehend. Something that fits well within their grand scheme of things. This notion of some quiet, yet strong and well educated person trying to establish an occupation such as clamming did not make any sense. The act of hand harvesting clams has and perhaps still is thought to be reserved for the recreational enthusiast who on nice occasions goes out with the Sunday barbecue in mind. Perhaps even the old school waterman who is simply trying to supplement their already meager income, or just the foolhardy. By most it is regarded as a base job. One requiring very little start up capital and little if any prior experience. Experience will come quickly to anyone brave and persistent enough to hand harvest clams as a profession. Other than your hands, there is no gear. No high tech navigational systems, or hydraulic machinery. An engine by which to move a boat is the only machine required. Perhaps even this could be debated. I have heard of a man living on Chincoteague Island who uses only a boat to get out to clamming grounds on a fairly regular basis. He uses the outgoing tide to get there and the incoming tide to get back. Granted this would only work when the weather and tides are in your favor. Though the tide at times can move very swiftly, especially in the narrow channels surrounding Chincoteague, the wind if strong enough and pushing against it can either halt the tides movement or even reverse its direction. I would imagine that the man from Chincoteague who clams without a motor has a great deal of patience, takes enough supplies to stay out there for several days, and carries a large paddle. The tide moves deceptively fast. Mostly because of the pull of the moon on fair wind days. According to Maxwell it can be used as a highway for traveling. One need only stay in the middle of the current to take maximum advantage of it. It took several years before Maxwell learned this.

CHAPTER II

THE SEARCH

There is an art to finding clams. One not only has to know where to look for them but as well how and when to look for them. Despite popular belief a clam does move. Not so much on a horizontal plane but rather on a vertical one giving them the ability to disappear into mud or sand almost without a trace. If it were not for the occasional dimple or keyhole created by a clams downward movement you would never even know they were their.

Maxwell who years before learned how to spot these holes, or "sign for clams" as locals call it, later gave it up and opted for a technique known as wading. To wade for clams a person simply walks through the water on a low tide feeling for clams with their feet. A light soled or non-soled shoe is recommended such that the round shell of a clam can easily be felt. However, Maxwell soon gave up these for a sturdier pair of running shoes. Oysters growing wild in the marsh tend to play havoc with anything one is wearing, especially footgear. A man named Joe, whom Maxwell has known since coming to the Shore wears a type of thick neoprene bootie. According to Joe, they do not last long either, but they can be fixed rather easily with rubber cement. Joe is an old school clammer, who still goes out on a fairly routine basis, all year long. Perhaps the arduous nature of the work has kept Joe fit at an age when most people are starting to use canes or walkers. Joe's passion for finding clams and oysters would rival even that of Maxwell's.

I would venture a guess many of the locals living on the Eastern Shore (last 100 years), are well versed at finding clams. The Chesapeake Bay Bridge has only been in existence for about 50 years. They have only been making highway bridges since the early 1900's. This would mean that the Eastern Shore of Virginia has been virtually isolated from the rest of the U.S. less than 100 years ago. My point is locals have their roots in clamming, learned here and nowhere else. Perhaps even subsistence wise, and some of them have learned the art of finding clams from knowledge passed down centuries ago. History always has a way of repeating itself.

Maxwell does not boast to be a better clammer than some of the locals, only one very interested in their solitary behavior and selfless existence.

Once clams are found with the feet, Maxwell settles down into the mud or sand, usually on all fours, and begins the task of feeling for them with his hands. When they are felt with the hands, they are quickly whisked into a bag kept by Maxwell's side. Once the bag is full it is simply hoisted onto one shoulder and carried back to the boat. If you clam in guts like Maxwell, this carry can at times be as much as a mile or more. Generally considering the small window of time in which a clammer can work on a low tide, this whole process has to occur very rapidly in order to make any money.

It should be mentioned that Maxwell has modified the technique of wading clams to include his hands in the initial search. In fact it would not be unusual to see Maxwell completely immersed in the water, with the exception of his head. That is at least during the warmer months of the year. This technique known by Maxwell as "full body wading", is easier on the back, allows one to stay cooler, and provides less exposed skin for hungry insects.

Including ones hands in the initial search for clams can play havoc both with ones gloves and ones mind. Maxwell's tenure as a teacher almost came to an end before it started because of the required fingerprinting that he had to undergo. Maxwell has no discernible fingerprints. His explanation of using his hands to clam with, constantly rubbing them on the bottom when searching, was met with both scrutiny and downright disbelief. After all, what better way for a criminal to remain anonymous than to remove their fingerprints. Maxwell was not a criminal, but perhaps he was being criminalized. Again, people will believe what is the easiest and/or most convenient to comprehend. Who in their right mind would subject their hands to such abuse. According to Maxwell, pushing and pulling ones hands through the top layer of mud and sand, provides the most efficient way of catching clams. He has tried rakes and picks, but invariably leaves them behind, often losing them, to use his hands only. Heaven only knows how many pairs of gloves he has been through. Several weeks often pass between the time his fingers go through and replacing them with another pair. During the interim his fingers take a beating. Especially from razor sharp oyster shells.

Aside from the abrasive bottom, Maxwell's hands are often plunged into deep, dark water. Unable to see what he is trying to grab, he will often mistake the smooth, round shell of a clam for a crab, fish, skate, stingray, turtle, or even eel. Believe it or not, an eel often poses the greatest problems. If disturbed they have a tendency to become aggressive. As well, sharks often frequent areas where Maxwell works. He has never been attacked by a shark, though working the edge of a wide channel one day he was circled by one.

It is not a job for the faint of heart. At times it takes summoning all of his courage to brave nature and her elements. If it were not for the inherent risks involved Maxwell would have probably chosen another profession. These very risks can also give value and appreciation to ones life. Perhaps the seemingly benign nature of clamming causes some people to let their guards down, thus accounting for an inordinate number of deaths each year.

Nature is in charge out there. According to Maxwell if this one premise is broken, disaster will soon follow. Generally speaking, staying safe out there is just a question of respect. Respect for where you are and what you are doing.

At first glance, when one looks at how easy it is to go out to the islands and dig for clams in a serene location with pleasant weather, it would hardly seem like work at all. This would be true for the recreational clammer who can pick and choose those pleasant days on which to go out. The commercial clammer is not afforded this luxury, and must constantly clam in order to put food on the table and to hold onto local markets with consistent prices. This would mean going out at all times of the year. In Winter when outside temperatures are near freezing and in Summer when horseflies and greenhead flies can torment both the mind and the body.

Before coming to the Shore, Maxwell lived in Alaska for two years and spent time working for the Bureau of Land Management. He was stationed in a small, former gold mining town, situated approximately 250 miles north of Tok. Basically, out in the middle of no where. Part of his job there was to provide assistance to motorists who either had accidents or were lost on the road (the one and only) that zigzagged its way along the 40 mile river corridor up to Eagle. Maxwell can tell you that most of the motorists never left their vehicles, and those that did quickly dove back in when they saw the hordes of hungry flies and mosquitoes waiting for them. I have heard entire herds of caribou will literally change migratory directions and head for the coast when the waves of insects are at their worst. The prevailing offshore winds would give them respite. The growing season in Alaska is much shorter than it is in the lower latitudes such as Virginia. With shorter growing seasons one sees tremendous explosions of vegetative growth and along with it multitudes of insects in the Summer. Though the sheer number of airborne insects might be fewer down here, the flies on the Shore are bigger and capable of taking a larger chunk of flesh from ones skin. Additionally, if your skin is salty, such as when you work in the marsh, you are even more desirable to a flies palate. Fresh water periodically doused on ones skin seems to work as well as any insect repellent that Maxwell has tried, regardless of the DEET content. As well, perhaps through natural selection, a mutant strain of fly has developed here with characteristics that allow them to know exactly where to bite you without being killed. This would be right in the middle of your back. Unless you are a contortionist or are constantly swatting them with say your shirt, gives the flies freedom to feast with relative abandon.

This brings me to the point of mentioning a key ability that Maxwell relies on while clamming in the Summer. The ability to still the mind and focus with absolute clarity. Kind of like tuning into a radio station. Everyone has this ability, few take advantage of it. If this can be done while wading for clams in the marsh, life will suddenly get easier. Even on those hot and sticky days when there seems to be no relief from the relentless waves of flies. On a physical level, when the mind is calm, your body temperature and blood pressure are lower. Excitation from a person can elicit the same degree of excitation from a fly and does nothing more than to trigger a feeding frenzy with any fly that is in your vicinity. It would seem that calming the mind almost makes you invisible, or at least, not as apparent to the fly. Almost as if you were blending in with everything around you.

As mentioned knowing how to clam is only part of the game. Being in the right place at the right time is the other.

Clams seem to be social animals. At least, they tend to be found in aggregate groups. In other words, if you find one, you will find many others. These clusters or jags as Maxwell calls them, can be anywhere from the size of a dinner plate to the size of a swimming pool if you are working in a large flat (level area of mud and/or sand that drops out high and dry on a low tide). Maxwell has even seen guts completely filled with clams from one end to the other.

The wild clam seems to prefer edges to establish themselves on. This could also only be a function of Maxwell not being able to reach clams in deep water without dredging equipment. An Eastern Shore waterman once told Maxwell that he welded a makeshift patent tong dredge onto his boat and started working the middle of wide channels and deeper guts. He was coming home everyday with a boat full of clams. His profits were tremendous. At least that is until word got around. Apparently it is illegal to do this. If my memory serves me correctly, the first time he was caught he was warned, the second time he was fined. I believe there are certain areas where it is still legal to do this. However most of the water between the mainland and the Barrier Islands are off limits to dredging. It would not be hard to imagine entire generations (all sizes) of clams never being touched, or seen for that matter, by humans. Clams by nature are filter feeders and thereby purify the water. Given this, maybe it is just as well that dredging them, at least on public ground, remain off limits.

Currents seem to play a role with where you find clams. The faster the current, the greater the number. That is, up to a point. If the current is too strong, the young clam will be washed away before it has ever had a chance to establish itself. Though a clam does not permanently attach itself to something like an oyster, it does like to generally stay in the same place. As mentioned, a clams movement is limited to up and down rather than sideways. Theoretically, a stronger current would provide a clam with a greater amount and wider assortment of food. As well, stronger currents increase the amount of oxygen in the water.

There are also more subtle indicators of where one can best find clams. Green sea lettuce found in a gut seems to be one. Both sea lettuce and clams have a sort of symbiotic relationship going on. Both organisms increase the amount of oxygen in the water and both need plenty of oxygen to survive.

When Maxwell first started clamming he seemed to be clueless on where to go. One day he heard reports from local watermen about bullfish (stingrays) ravaging planted clam beds. It seemed logical that clams could also be found in the wild by noticing where large schools of stingrays tended to congregate at. A short time later working in an area out of Quinby he noticed the telltale sign of wingtips breaking the surface of the water around a large tump (marsh island). They were stingrays feeding on clams around the perimeter of this island. Maxwell also started clamming in this area. Clams were so numerous here that he went back to the same place for the better part of the summer.

Of any creature, including man, a stingray would represent the most efficient clam hunter of them all. Their ability to extract and devour clams off the bottom almost seems to be effortless and is certainly unrivalled. Maxwell has watched these fish up close underwater in the wild. A stingray will gently flap its wings just off the bottom, stirring up the sand and silt enough to expose clams that were once hidden. Once exposed, they are sucked up into their mouths where the meat is devoured and the shell spit back out. All of this is done very quickly and efficiently while the stingray is still moving forward. When clams are found a stingray becomes much like a free ranging vacuum cleaner. Even chowder size clams are no match for their massive jaws.

Other fish as well can be good indicators of where to find clams. One winter, as Maxwell was pushing his boat out from a beach into deeper water around an inlet, he noticed a large number of small black dorsal fins breaking the surface. In fact, almost churning it up. Upon closer inspection, he realized that it was a large school of black drum fish. They were out there doing the same thing he was. Looking for clams. Except they were in deeper water and working the sandy edge of the inlet. As Maxwell was standing within arms reach of perhaps hundreds of black drum, he knew that if he had brought along a net, clams would not be the only thing he would be taking home that day.

Eventually most clammers including Maxwell, simply go back to the same areas over and over again. These areas for whatever reason, have always supported large numbers of clams and can be worked periodically for an indefinite time. In general, Maxwell only works the top layer of the bottom, allowing clams underneath to grow and reproduce. This provides for a sustainable harvest year in and year out. As a rule, only topneck (middle size) clams are sought out, allowing smaller clams to grow bigger, and allowing bigger clams to reproduce. Theoretically, a clam is hermaphroditic, giving it the ability to change sex during the course of its life. A clam will start out as a male and then change to female after a period of 1 to 2 years. There is some debate on this topic. I don't think enough research has been done to know for sure. In any case, by leaving both small and large clams, one appears to allow both sexes to stay within the population and consequently to perpetuate themselves. According to Maxwell, this has always seemed to work. Larger clams in addition to being female, are also more prolific spawners or bigger egg producers. When Maxwell worked as a scientist, he at times counted as many as 10 million eggs produced from only a single clam. Considering the size of the egg cell, they are fairly easy to see. It should be mentioned that larger clams, in addition to being massive egg producers, have also had time to build up immunity to an entire host of diseases. By leaving larger clams one is, in effect, allowing for a more disease resistant population to develop.

The general search for only topneck clams also works from an economic perspective. Topneck clams command the highest market prices. People seem to prefer this size to any other. Perhaps this is because there is simply not enough meat in a smaller clam, and a larger clam has to be cut up for preparation in dishes.

The search for a clam also involves timing. As mentioned, there is a relatively small amount of time that one can clam by hand. To put it simply, the water has to be low enough to reach them. This translates into only being able to work when the water is roughly two and a half foot deep or less. About the length of your arm, if you are an adult.

Maxwell prefers to leave the dock on an outgoing tide. It is easier on the engine and you burn less gas. He tries to arrive at the particular clamming spot a couple of hours before the tide has reached its lowest point. This gives him two hours before the low tide and two hours after to work. Some days there is more time and some days less. It all depends on what the tide is doing that particular day. Maxwell will generally start working at the head (place where the gut ends) and slowly make his way towards the mouth (place where the gut starts and adjoins a larger channel). The head of a gut has the highest elevation and consequently the least amount of water. In general, smaller clams are found here. Why this is, Maxwell is not sure. He can only postulate that it has something to do with a slower current. The clams can more readily stay in the same place where they were first established. It remains one of the mystery's of the marsh.

Maxwell has seen days when the tide has dropped so low and stayed out for so long that he has been able to work from sunrise to sunset. Unfortunately these days are few and far between. Most days he is fortunate to get between 4 and 6 hours of actual working time in. Many factors play into what the tide will do on any given day. Some of these would include, the intensity and direction of the wind, the moon's position relative to the earth, the amount of rainfall received, and even storms off the coast which can produce what are known as tidal surges. Knowing what a tide will do perhaps comes as much from experience as it does from simply looking at local tide charts and weather forecasts. The tide, like most things in the marsh, is very unpredictable. One would think that at times it has a mind of its own, or at least follows its own agenda. Perhaps this is part of the allure. Maxwell has always admired the wildness of the marsh. Otherwise, it would be just another boring job. It seems with each new day comes a new adventure.

In Winter, the risk of getting hypothermia seems to be a constant threat. The very notion of maintaining ones body temperature at or near 98.6 becomes an act of attrition. There is a unique cost. Namely that of jeopardizing ones life every time the boat leaves the dock. I suppose all fishermen do, or at least should, understand this risk.

There are a few extra precautions that Maxwell makes a point to follow when he is out half-wading for clams when both the water and air temperature are very cold. First, one does not want to get wet. At least, not your upper body. It is normal for the lower part of Maxwell's legs to get wet as soon as he steps off the boat into the marsh. Again as long as the torso stays warm and dry, the rest of the body will follow suit. As well, you can stay out of the water long enough to warm up your hands by sticking them down your chestwaders, if you are fortunate to have them, your pants if you don't, or even under your armpits, before reentering the water for another 20-30 minute spell. Secondly, always bring a dry change of clothes for the unexpected, or just something to change into for the boat ride back home. Thirdly, Maxwell always tries to carry a butane lighter, at least on the boat, every time he goes out. It could save your life. There is a lot of driftwood out there, especially on the higher spots in the marsh. Places that Maxwell frequents. These higher areas are easier to walk in because the ground is firmer.

There is something in the marsh that Maxwell likes to call quickmud. Almost everyone has seen, or at least heard of quicksand. But few would admit having even heard of quickmud. This is a soft conglomeration of mud and silt that one often finds in the lower areas of the marsh. Maxwell has stepped into it on more than one occasion. One must try to make their body as light as possible to get out of it. After many years of tramping in the marsh, Maxwell has learned to identify quickmud from a distance so that it can be more easily avoided. If one stands in the middle of quickmud for very long they will continue sinking. How far, Maxwell does not know, nor does he want to find out.

One time Maxwell was clamming in an area that seemed to be surrounded in this quickmud. He was completely absorbed in his work and therefore did not at first hear the muffled call from a person that seemed to be in distress. After all, who in their right mind would even be in the same place that Maxwell often clammed in. After several minutes of disregarding the sound, or at least passing it off for the sound of the wind or a distant boat, he decided to stand up, get on higher ground, and afford himself a better view. In the distance towards the east he noticed a lone boat and what appeared to be a lone person stuck up to their neck in mud. It turned out that the person in question was a state game warden, obviously a rookie, and not at all acquainted with the marsh and its peculiar characteristics. He was in a good pocket of quickmud, and the more he struggled to get out, the further down he went. Upon closer inspection the lone boat turned out to be the Coast Guard who had taken this warden out here to check the licenses of hunters apparently shooting black ducks well off in the distance. I guess the warden regarded the walk to get to these hunters as nothing more than a mere stroll through the park. To say the least, he was unpleasantly surprised. With all the weight he was carrying (guns, flashlight, etc.), I was not surprised at what happened. Maxwell rushed over to him and within a few minutes pulled him onto firmer ground.

As previously mentioned, to walk through the marsh with any degree of efficiency, one must become as light as possible. And one must never stand still, especially when in quickmud. The ability for one to become as light as possible, is not a concept readily understood. Perhaps the best way to explain it would be to use the analogy of cross country skiing. The mechanics of cross country skiing and walking through the marsh are much the same. To stay on top of the snow, a skier must project the body upwards while still moving forward. At the same time, the feet must be shuffled or slid along the surface instead of being lifted. This combined action, at least momentarily, makes the body lighter. The physical properties of wet mud and that of snow are very similar. Given Maxwell's past experience as a cross country ski instructor, he seemed to be right at home. It should be mentioned that though this technique for walking through the marsh, if done right, seems to be effortless, it is not. It requires great strength and great stamina. I have heard of a man who one year won the gold medal for a cross country skiing endurance race held at the Winter Olympics in Calgary, Canada. He not only won the race but apparently blew away the field shattering records along the way. I further learned that he trained for this event by simply slogging through the swamp bottomland on foot, in his hometown where he grew up.

In the Winter months, especially during the early years of clamming, there were on occasion close calls that are forever etched in Maxwell's memory. One day Maxwell went out to look for clams at the head of a cut-through about 5 miles from the mainland. As he was working in a gut a heavy fog set in. He barely had enough time to get back to his boat before losing sight of it. As he was in the boat the fog became so heavy that he could not make out the navigational beacons marking the edge of a channel that he needed to take to get back in. Worried about having to spend the night there, he decided to make a run for it. A boat run back across a very large and very shallow bay. If one does not stay in the channel at the western end of Bradford Bay (see map insert) on a low tide, they will run aground. The tide was still low when Maxwell started across. By the time he was about halfway across the fog became so thick that he could not see the hand in front of his face. To make matters worse, the sun was setting and it was cold. Maxwell slowed the boat down almost to an idle, pointed the bow in the direction that he thought he needed to go, and hoped for the best. By the grace of God, he did not hit anything and no one was coming at him. However, he wound up missing the dock from where he started by about 2 miles. And just in the nick of time, before running aground on the western shore, he caught a glimpse of the only thing that gave him any indication as to where he was. A flashing red navigational beacon. Only because of this, he finally made it back to the dock at about 11 that night. Maxwell has never before or since, seen the fog set in so quickly and so heavily.

Outboard motors, as one would expect, play a vital role in the search for clams. If they become inoperable or do not function properly, the search for clams becomes limited. Since the time he started clamming, Maxwell has been through a great number of outboards. Everything from old Evinrudes/ Johnsons (same thing), to Yamahas and Mercury's. Some of them went underwater while the boat was at the dock. The boats either got hung up on something and were pulled under, or high winds flipped the boat over. Each time happening when Maxwell was not there. One particular outboard ended up going underwater 3 times in the span of about a year. Maxwell managed to pull it out each time, drain the saltwater out, clean it, lubricate it, and restart it. The trick is to never let them sit too long when they first come out of the water. The saltwater immediately begins to corrode the metal when the outboard is exposed to the air. Metal corrodes because of a process known as oxidation. Oxidation, to my knowledge, does not occur underwater. Theoretically, it is possible for an outboard to still work if it is underwater even for a couple days. Once Maxwell managed to right a boat that had flipped at the dock in high winds. He bailed it out, drained the motor, cleaned it, and lubricated it while it was still attached. He then started it and went clamming. All in the same day. Unfortunately, the more times an outboard goes underwater the greater the chance that irreparable damage will be done. Internal parts begin to seize up. Maxwell has found that the best way to keep an outboard functioning at it's best is to simply run it everyday. Even just exposed to the salt air, an outboard can become damaged if it is not run.

There was an incident with an outboard once that Maxwell will never forget. This particular outboard had been experiencing transmission difficulties for about a week prior to the incident. Inadvertently coming out of gear while running, or not going into gear seemed to be routine with this outboard. One day in January, Maxwell was out clamming and he was not paying close enough attention to the time and the fact that it was starting to get dark. He was catching clams and decided to keep working as long as possible even if it meant running back in after the sun dipped below the horizon. There is still enough light to see a little, even after this point. Unfortunately this was also the time when the minor outboard transmission problem became a major one. The motor simply refused to go into forward gear. It appeared that the lower unit was in the process of seizing up. By now, it was completely dark and Maxwell realized that if he did not get back in that he was in for a very long and very cold night. He had forgotten to bring along his heavy jacket. After several minutes of swearing, followed by fervent prayer for forgiveness, Maxwell found that he could at least put the outboard in reverse gear. As well, it would stay in this gear, as long as he was running very slowly. Considering the stillness of the night, and the amount of light coming from a full moon, Maxwell decided to chance backing the boat the entire way back to the dock. Keep in mind, this was a small, open boat, about 14' long, with a low profile stern. If the weather had decided to get nasty, nothing would have prevented the water from coming in. Also, if Maxwell had run aground going backwards, there is a good chance that the stern transom would have broken off completely. With a long swim in any direction, in the middle of January, this particular incident seemed to have all the earmarks for disaster. Somehow, Maxwell managed to keep the boat in the middle of the channel using a form of dead reckoning to constantly determine his position. If Maxwell was a cat, he would have used up 3 of his 9 lives on this one.

The search for clams often involves having as much patience waiting for things to happen, as it does having perseverance trying to make things happen. There was a time many Winters ago, when Maxwell went out clamming and decided to go to a point of land near Wachapreague Inlet (see map insert). There is a lot of open water out here and it is deep in the middle. The wind was blowing 15-20 mph when he left the dock. It is always good practice to make sure that you put your boat in a place where if it is blowing hard, the boat will be pushed away from land instead of towards it. In other words, only put your boat up to leave it on the lee side of an island. Either Maxwell was simply not thinking early in the morning, or the wind shifted while Maxwell was out tramping in the marsh. For whatever reason, by the time Maxwell returned to the boat with a bag of clams, the wind was increasing and was pushing the boat towards land. Maxwell remembers grabbing a large Danforth anchor and heaving it off the boat repeatedly until the boat was in deep enough water such that the motor could be put down. The water was cold and Maxwell did not want to chance getting completely wet by dragging the boat to deep water. Between the engine refusing to start and the anchor refusing to hold, the situation seemed to get worse. Every time Maxwell stopped heaving the anchor long enough to put the motor down and try to start it, the wind pushed the boat back towards the beach. In high winds, without enough scope (angle that the line is going in the water), the anchor becomes useless. This went on for a couple of hours, until finally the tides helped out and Maxwell could put the motor down right where he was, and right where he had stayed the entire time. So much extra effort for nothing. Maxwell should have simply waited. You cannot fight Mother Nature. Every time Maxwell has tried to fight her, he has miserably failed. She decides everything out here. Maxwell now only uses a long metal pole pushed directly into the mud to hold the boat. With one good line, attached on one end to the bow of the boat, the other end attached to the bottom of the pole, there is no better anchor for around here. It has taken many years for Maxwell to learn this, in the process almost losing his boat, but it has been learned.

Speaking of losing one's boat. This has only been done once by Maxwell. And this particular time was in the summer. As well, it was not a question of the anchor not holding, but rather a question of not being able to find the boat because of thick fog. It is hard enough at times trying to find a boat in tall marsh grass with ample light, let alone in the fog. As mentioned the fog can set in very quickly out here. On this particular day, Maxwell had Jim, the mud dog. Jim usually stayed within 4 or 5 yards of Maxwell in the marsh. He had been trained to do this from an early age. Maxwell always seemed to get a peace of mind from just having Jim around. Besides, having an extra pair of eyes and a good nose for tracking, Jim usually made finding the boat that much easier.

One day, Maxwell seemed to get so absorbed into his work, deep within a gut, that he was not paying attention to the fog that started creeping up very slowly all around him. Maxwell stood up suddenly, got on the highest point he could find, looked out and saw nothing. After collecting his thoughts and finding Jim nearby, he simply went back into the gut and continued trying to find clams. The eyes are not necessary anyways. After an hour or so, the fog let up enough such that Maxwell could get some idea of where he was.

The fog, if thick enough, can render one completely disoriented. If it were not for gravity holding your feet on the ground, you would have no idea of what is up, down, or sideways. As with heavy rain squalls, severe lightning storms, and sometimes heavy wind, it is usually best to stay put and wait it out. Like many places, the more severe the weather is on the Shore, the more short-lived it will also be. That is with the exception of large fronts, such as nor'easters, which can take as long as a week to pass over. These fronts can, and should be, predicted well in advance, such that they can be avoided entirely. It becomes a simple question of checking local forecasts. In any case, Maxwell never leaves the dock now without at least being prepared to stay out there for an indefinite period. You can hope for the best, but be prepared for the worst. You never really know what the weather will do here. Sometimes even from one hour to the next.

Maxwell still remembers a few years back when he went out to Cedar Island (see map insert) to try and work two tides. The low tide at night when the sun was going down, and the low tide the next morning, when the sun was coming up. Working both tides like this can save time and gas expenditures. As well, it can often mean making twice as much money. The only criteria being, one must spend the night out there.

On this particular occasion, all did not go in Maxwell's favor. A large storm from the north blew in that night and soon wind gusts averaged somewhere in the 30-50 mph range. According to later reports, someone mistook a flashing red light for Maxwell's boat as he was leaving that night. They evidently called the Coast Guard to go and investigate. At around 11 that evening Maxwell and his dog Jim were woken from a restless sleep by the sound of a huge helicopter doing a low aerial search pattern from the air. The search light they were using eventually was shining directly on Maxwell's tent, located on high ground, just about in the middle of this long and narrow island. It reminded Maxwell of a scene from "Close Encounters of the Third Kind", when a giant UFO hovers over a small house. In this case it was a large Coast Guard transport chopper. When it finally landed nearby Maxwell was more concerned for his tent being blown away from the wash of the helicopter blades than from the winds of the storm. A navy seal prepared for a water rescue appeared from the darkness and asked Maxwell if he was alright. Maxwell told him he was fine, appreciated his concern, and would stay the night. At around 3 am that morning, the winds were too strong for his tent to stay upright. He packed everything up and with Jim by his side literally crawled along the sand in the dark to a section of the island that could afford a better break from the winds. The winds were still strong when the sun finally came up. Maxwell decided to work the tide anyways, although just around his boat, which he intentionally and very fortunately left in a protected cove on the lee side of the island. By around noon that day winds were diminished somewhat though still hazardous for small craft travel. Maxwell had other things to do that day, so he decided to chance it and try to make his way back in. Besides, he was looking at spending a couple more nights there if he didn't. Everything went okay until he started across a stretch at a place called Sandy Point. He remembers hitting a large rogue wave. All of the clams that he had stored in the bow to balance the boat out came sliding down to him and his dog Jim, causing the entire boat to point straight up in the air. Keep in mind, at the time, his boat was a 12', shallow draft, open skiff. Maxwell grabbed Jim and leapt forward, somehow preventing the entire boat from completely turning over. Considering the amount of water now in the boat, if he had been hit by another wave at this point, the story would have never been told. When Maxwell finally got back to the dock, he was berated by other fishermen for not using better judgment in going out in such severe weather. The weather on the Eastern Shore is very fickle and best laid plans can quickly go awry at a moments notice. When Maxwell first left on this trip, the weather was picture perfect. No one, including the people making the local forecasts predicted the storm that was to follow. Running into bad weather is kind of like running aground. If you haven't done both it simply means that you haven't been working on the water long enough.

Chapter III

Maxwell's House

I think if one tries to define the word house they invariably run the risk of oversimplifying a not so simple word. First, it has so many definitions. Eighteen, according to the dictionary; "American Heritage Dictionary" (1975 ed.).

Secondly, though the word itself lacks ambiguity; everyone knows what a house is; the context in which house is used is highly variable. And the context itself can add subtle variations to the definition of the word.

According to Maxwell, a house is much more than just a physical place. Metaphorically, it is a structured dwelling that is occupied as much in the mind as it is in the body. It is the one thing that all people will spend an entire lifetime trying to build, or at least maintain. It can be knocked down or damaged quite easily. But it can be rebuilt or repaired, sometimes as easily. This house will invariably last if it is built upon a solid foundation.

Since arriving on the Shore, the place most occupied by Maxwell has been the marsh. In body when he is there, in spirit when he is not. In essence it is his house. It is both the place where he feels the most protected, and the place that he feels the most need to protect. It is a house known by many, yet understood by very few.

By and large, the marsh is regarded as a formidable place. Full of unknown creatures and besieged by great storms that come through its unprotected realms. We humans by nature, often fear what we do not understand. It is unbuildable, unwalkable, and in the process of constantly changing. It never stays still. Not fit for human habitation, it is to many, simply undesirable. Pleasing to the eye from a distance, but only from a distance. Once in it, most people get the unnerving sensation of being held in place or even pulled down.

Perhaps all of this can be a good thing. Do you think for one minute that this marsh, with all its pristine beauty and original splendor, untouched for the most part since the day it was established, would have remained so if it were readily accessible? I do not. It would be changed. How exactly I do not know, but in a way that would better accommodate man. If there is one trait universal to all mankind, it is having control over ones dominion. Whatever dominion that might be. When we do not feel we have control, even over nature, we will still try to get it. Just look at what the Army Corp of Engineers is doing with the Mississippi River. We might someday see man's incessant need for control even in the marsh. It will start with the subtle form of walkways, made of materials impervious to salt damage, crisscrossing the marsh landscape wherever you turn. I hope not, but I suppose it is possible. Until then, Maxwell will continue to enjoy its raw and dynamic beauty.

The foundation on which Maxwell's house is built can be thought of as prior knowledge gained through both formal education and past work experience. As mentioned, one of Maxwell's former occupations was that of a scientist. He worked as a Lab Technician for the Virginia Institute of Marine Science, Eastern Shore Lab, in Wachapreague, Virginia. He loved the job. It seemed that he was in his element working with shellfish. The wages however left something to be desired, so after his seasonal contract was over, he decided to call it quits.

Maxwell had spent many years trying to perfect the craft of raising clams indoors. Upon arriving on the Shore, he read anything and everything about clams that he could get his hands on. He networked with people who were either directly or indirectly associated with clam hatcheries. He even worked for several clam growers in the area around which he lived.

After about five years of learning how other people did it, Maxwell thought it was time to put a clam hatchery together of his own design. It would be a small scale, biointensive, closed recirculation-type system (see hatchery layout). The only other person who helped in the hatchery was Joe. According to Maxwell, both he and Joe became nothing more than glorified janitors after everything was set up and operational. One does not have the benefits of the tide to constantly wash away built up sediment and detritus from the bottoms of the trays and tanks. All of this has to be done manually and on a consistent basis, otherwise clams will perish.

At the time, if one were to walk from the north end to the south end of the hatchery building they would have seen 5, 5 gallon algal containers, each growing an algae colony under fluorescent lighting. This was food for the clams. The algae stock originally came from the Eastern Shore Lab where Maxwell had worked. Like making bread, it helps to have a starter.

Once an algal colony starts growing, it perpetuates itself. Continuing south in the building, one would have seen an 800 gallon tank that was designed to contain larvae from the initial spawn, up until the clams were catching (staying on top of) a 250 micron or larger mesh screen. The clams were then moved to shallow recirculation trays located on the south end of the building. When not filled with larvae, the 800 gallon tank became an extra container to grow algae in. The shallow trays were positioned next to south facing windows such that the sun could help heat the water. Keep in mind that the first spawn took place around the beginning of April when outside water temperatures are still quite cold.

The system was designed to grow algae concurrently with clams. The algae seemed to do well in this hatchery. Unfortunately, not as much can be said for the clams. Looking back, Maxwell now thinks that he was not separating out the sizes as much as he should have been. He simply did not have the space to do this. As well, even with the 800 gallon tank he was still not growing enough food to feed the clams. You can only imagine how much is eaten daily when you have between 500,000-750,000 small clams growing in a relatively small space. The same type of space/food constraints determine whether a clam will live or die in the wild. Maxwell has always said that a hatchery is not suppose to replace Mother Nature, only enhance it by speeding it up a little. Nature is still doing the work.

Timing in a hatchery is critical. Maxwell would bring wild clams out of the field as early as late March for spawning. About 2 dozen clams would be selected and placed in shallow trays. After running repeated cycles of warm and cold water through these trays there seemed to be no problem getting huge spawns. Maxwell would often arrive early in the morning to see a sort of light snow covering the bottom of the trays. This snow being unfertilized clam eggs.

A wild clam seems to be programmed to spawn every year right around the end of April up until the end of May. In fact, both clams and oysters have two spawns a year in the wild. One in the late spring as mentioned and one in the early fall, if you are on the Eastern Shore. The one in the spring, according to scientists, is the bigger of the two, and the one that Maxwell was trying to duplicate. The same regime of cold and warm water passing over a clams shell in the wild, triggers the spawning.

As mentioned, timing is crucial. Maxwell needed to have all clams growing out in the trays by the end of June. Otherwise, there would not be time to get everything up to a plantable size (6mm or larger) by September. Everything at this size was suppose to be taken out by boat and planted under nets on leased ground. It did not quite work out this way.

Despite the fact the hatchery was located in an area of poor water quality (next to a marina and a large storm drain), with inadequate supplies and outdated equipment, Maxwell still managed to produce around 50,000 plantable-sized seed clams his first year of operation. Suffice it to say, after the first year, things got worse before they got better. One morning Maxwell went in to find all of his post set clam seed either dead or in the process of dying. It would take writing another book to list all of the possible reasons. It was too late in the spring to attempt another spawn. So with around 15,000 dollars invested into a business that just did not seem to be working, Maxwell decided to call it quits, at least for the time being. Debts were mounting and he needed to pursue an occupation, where he could at least make money. Despite the apparent failure, much was learned about the wild clam from attempting to grow a cultured one. In effect the foundation for Maxwell's house had been established. The permanent occupants of this house, namely the clam and oyster, could be better understood. As well, in order to hunt a clam with any degree of success it helps to know a little about their natural history. Specifically, how they reproduce, where they live, how and what they eat, and what eats them. The information contained in this next section applies specifically to the hard clam, Mercenaria mercenaria and is relevant to all areas within the tidal marsh, from the mainland of the Eastern Shore out to the Barrier Islands. (see map)

A clam first makes its appearance in this world not as what we would recognize as a clam, but rather as a small veliger larva. This larva is mobile and is the result of one of millions of eggs spawned from a single female clam seasonally. The egg is fertilized by sperm from a male clam, present somewhere in the near vicinity. Cell division occurs and through a process known as gametogenesis, a single larva develops. All of this occurs within 24 hours after fertilization. At this point, the larva is free swimming and will try to find a place to establish itself. Unlike the oyster at this stage, it does not permanently attach itself to anything but rather burrows itself in the bottom, whatever bottom that might be. On the Eastern Shore one can find clams in silt, soft-aggregate such as right in the middle of an established oyster reef, in sand, soft or hard mud, clay, or any combination thereof. The veliger larvae are simply trying to find a place where they are free of predation and where there is ample food. Predation that I speak of comes from, but is not limited to, blue crabs, horseshoe crabs, certain fish such as black drum, and of course the stingray.

Of all predators, it is highly probable that the blue crab poses the greatest threat to a clam, at least early on in a clams growth. Anyone that raises clams under nets would provide testimony to this. If even a single crab is left under a net, or is somehow able to get under one, the losses to the clam grower can be immense. Maxwell has seen firsthand, entire beds measuring 20 by 60 foot, ravaged by crabs which will leave nothing in their wake besides small pieces of shell. Fortunately for the clam grower, a crabs jaws are only big enough to consume small seed size clams, (8mm or under).

A clam is known as a filter feeder. It ingests small food particles (algae) from the surrounding water via a siphon (foot) protruding from its shell. Nutrients from this food will be assimilated and stored by the clam leaving that which is undesirable or unabsorbable to be excreted out. This excretion known as pseudofeces often contain toxins or impurities from the water which are harmful to the clam as well as to the environment. In this sense, a clam can be looked at as a type of water purifier or waste treatment facilitator. By filter feeding, a clam in effect is increasing the amount of oxygen in the water while locking away harmful contaminants that might be present. It is very common to see minnows hovering in water, just off the bottom, where clams are burrowed. One gets the sense that they are merely enjoying the oxygen boost provided by the clams. In any case, by the simple act of feeding, a clam improves itself while also improving its surroundings. A sort of mutual symbiosis. Higher oxygen levels translate into better water clarity. Better clarity allows for more light to penetrate further down into the water column thus promoting the establishment and maintenance of underwater grasses. In turn, these grasses provide cover for crabs and fish. One begins to see a fine tuned, delicately balanced system. Moreover, if any of the components that comprise this system are removed, the system will not work. Conservation efforts will be in vain unless this is kept in mind. It is hard enough to even know all of the components that comprise a system, let alone to try to regulate any of them.

There is another element in all of this that comes to mind. The very idea of success in this country, perhaps everywhere, appears to be insidious and does not come without inherent cost. Success is not measured strictly in terms of monetary gain, or even in terms of what benefits can be derived in the here and now. If Maxwell were to go and completely strip an area of all of its clams, he would most certainly maximize profits now, but what would the costs be in terms of environmental degradation and monetary gain further down the road. The future would look bleak both for himself and others who rely on significant populations of clams to sustain already dwindling fisheries. And when I speak of fisheries, I speak of anything and everything that can be harvested from the water.

Anyone can be a clam hunter. One simply needs to go stumbling haphazardly through the marsh one day in search of clams. To be a good clam hunter entails a much greater degree of purpose, and with that respect for the environment. Perhaps this idea is never totally ingrained until one has spent a considerable number of years trying to make a living on the water. One begins to notice what they are leaving themselves. With all the new innovative ways that have come out lately with increasing the proficiency of harvesting seafood (greater yields with less work effort), maybe the idea of leaving enough of a resource to be sustained year in and year out, has been left by the wayside. Nowadays, most of the commercial fishermen that I am aware of are interested in trying to keep up with an ever burgeoning appetite for wild stock seafood while trying to circumvent ever tightening laws and restrictions imposed. As the demand continues to grow, the supply continues to decline. We are left with a commercial industry whose idea of success is born of having larger boats with greater storage holds and in some cases the capacity to process an entire marketable product before the boat even gets back to the dock. We are enamored with the high tech equipment and gear, including radar and satellite navigation, enabling one to get to a particular area much faster and efficiently than before. My point is we are only interested in catching more now, without a plan for sustaining future stocks. With regulations being tightened (both federal and state), it is more important than ever for the commercial fisherman to increase efficiency. Those that don't seem to follow the course of being regulated right out of business. To catch as much as one can as quickly as one can. Depending on the type and amount of gear one fishes with, this idea could very well help determine the amount of time it takes for a fishery to become depleted. There is no singular cause for a fisheries demise. Many factors come into play and all share part of the blame. Everything from the increasing number of recreational fishermen to the overflowing septic tank in ones backyard.

Perhaps if the clam and oyster industry on the Eastern Shore were to ever fade away, it would not be without first being replaced by some other shellfish. Something able to out compete the clam and oyster within it's own niche, and something that is simply worth the effort to put on ones plate.

According to Maxwell, a clam is one of nature's perfect foods. Eaten raw, preferably with horseradish, there is nothing better to sustain ones energy while clamming in the marsh. What better reason to help protect it.

A clam's full value will never be completely recognized. Suffice it to say, it is an integral part of Maxwell's house. A house over which people preside as mere custodians.

Chapter IV

Mud Dog Jim

Maxwell has now seen many years go by without his faithful friend, First Mate, and companion Jim. He was a yellow lab, and looked like one, though his mother was a full bred Siberian Husky. He was smart and was raised by Maxwell from the time he was weaned. After coming to the Shore he, like Maxwell, soon became well acquainted with the marsh. He was appropriately named mud dog because of his tendency to enter the marsh as a yellow lab and come out looking like a brown one. Both he and Maxwell shared a common affinity for the marsh while tramping through it.

The days were rare when the two were not seen together. The first year, it was basically the blind leading the blind. Neither had a clue as to what they were doing or where they were going. After a while however, they both soon walked with a greater degree of purpose and direction.

As Maxwell wanted to maintain a steady market for his clam harvesting and bring in a continual income, the days when the weather was just too miserable or unsafe, became few and far between. He became determined to try and maintain a commercial fisherman's livelihood. He loved it and as he often said, it seemed to fit him like a glove. Other than following the direction of tides and weather, he had no one telling him what to do, he could work as long or as little as he so chose, and he could venture into places of his own choosing. How many people can boast of such freedom with their job.

Most, if not all, things Maxwell ever started eventually worked themselves into acts of obsession. I have never been sure as to whether this is a good or bad thing. There are few people who actually clam for a living, and even fewer who will do it on bitter cold, even raw days in the middle of winter. Maxwell was one of these people.

As part of a daily routine in the clammer's world, Jim had been trained to jump into Maxwell's truck or boat on command. Being of independent spirit like his master, he soon began doing this without even being told. Maxwell would simply have to open the truck door or pull the boat up to the dock. Unfortunately as well, it was not always just Maxwell's truck or boat. On occasion, Jim could be seen returning to the mainland in Joe's boat. Joe was very fond of Jim and often had a treat for him while working out on the islands. No matter, Maxwell trusted Joe, and he knew that Jim would always find a way back in.

One morning, as a light snow was falling, ensuring a cold, wet day to work in, neither Jim or Maxwell seemed to be in a hurry to head down to the boat. Opening the truck door seemed to make no difference to Jim. Even the command on this particular morning was ignored. After deliberating himself as to whether this day was even worth suffering through, Maxwell began noticing a funny limp develop in one of Jim's forelegs. Much like a killdeer feigning injury, Jim began hopping around pretending his leg was hurt. I think in this way he could enjoy the comfort of a nice, warm house while Maxwell stumbled around in the marsh. The only problem with Jim's plan was in maintaining which foot was actually hurt. I guess even he forgot and soon began hopping frantically from one foot to the other. Nevertheless, Maxwell got the message and left Jim behind that day. Though it was neither the first or the last time Maxwell found himself working alone in the winter, it was nice to have the companionship of a dog when the days can be very stark and dreary.

There were a few close calls that Maxwell and Jim shared together in the marsh. One afternoon in the summer they were out on Parramore Island working in a remote area, somewhere in the middle of the island. As they often do, a storm came up suddenly and before either knew it, lightning bolts seemed to be coming out of the sky all around them. Not wanting to be around the long metal pole sticking out of the ground to hold the boat, Maxwell decided to stay put where he was clamming at the time. For a few minutes both he and Jim pressed their bodies as close to the ground as they could get them. I'm not sure why. Lightning bolts were coming straight down anyways. Though it was short-lived, Maxwell has never before or since seen a lightning storm of such intensity. I believe Jim developed a long-term phobia of storms, even slight ones, on account of this particular day. As well, one of the bolts apparently hit the radio antenna at the old Coast Guard station situated on the northern end of the island. It started a fire that continued burning for months afterwards. You could stand in Wachapreague and watch the distant orange glow both night and day. When it finally went out, more than half the island had been consumed.

Even in the summer, aside from the companionship, Jim seemed to serve a special function. As mentioned, Maxwell often clammed in areas also frequented by sharks. Having two pairs of eyes instead of one to keep a lookout for them, seemed to at least provide a sense of security for Maxwell. Though I am not sure, I think Jim became well acquainted with sharks.

There was a particular episode one summer that Maxwell will never forget. One day, he and Jim were out at the extreme end of Parramore Island. As the crow flies, they were as far out as one can get from the mainland, while still being on the eastern fringes of the Barrier Islands. It had been a particularly hot and dry summer with temperatures at the time climbing to over 100 degrees in the noonday sun. After a day of clamming, Maxwell was in a hurry to get home, especially considering the catch that day consisted mostly of chowders, the largest size clams. The weight of a chowder is roughly three times greater than that of a topneck. This consideration, along with getting about half as much money per clam, hardly makes searching for chowders even worth the effort. It seemed that this was all Maxwell could find in this particular place at this particular time. At around 4 or 5 that afternoon Maxwell decided to head on in. Not only had he spent a lot of gas and time getting here, he wound up making little money in the process.

Chowders seem to have a more difficult time in the sun than the smaller clams. The main abductor muscle which acts to continually keep the shell of a clam closed is relaxed. When out of the water, this muscle is seldom relaxed, especially when an element such as heat is compromising its very survival. Once the shell opens in the hot sun, it is only a matter of minutes before the meat inside spoils. Clams were popping open everywhere.

On this day, as clams were being stressed, so to was Maxwell, especially considering that Jim was no where around the boat and he needed to get in to save what was left of his catch. Jim often liked to wander on his own in the marsh and at the time he was too far from the boat to hear Maxwell's beckoning calls or he was too afraid to come near it. Considering Maxwell's increasing agitation, it would be no wonder if Jim was even being driven further from the boat. All of this went on for another 2 or 3 hours. The sun was now getting ready to set. At this point, any further attempt to get Jim back seemed in vain. Maxwell, on the verge of an anxiety breakdown finally decided to head back in without his partner. Tears were in his eyes as he gunned the motor, silently vowing to return at first light the next morning. Maxwell's conscience has always been his guide, and he knew he would never forgive himself if Jim was not later found. Unfortunately the next morning, Jim was no where to be seen. Finding a yellow lab amongst tall, yellow marsh grass, was like trying to find a needle in a haystack. Constant searching turned up nothing. Maxwell even climbed onto the roof of an old hunting shack to get a better vantage point. Still nothing. His searching increased. He was coming back to the same spot, where Jim was last seen, now both in the morning and in the evening. Still nothing. Four days later, Maxwell came in after another fruitless search for Jim, only to find a worn out and dehydrated dog waiting for him at the dock. It was as if a great weight were suddenly lifted from Maxwell's shoulders. Jim was back. To this day, Maxwell thanks God for sparing him from the burden of guilt. Apparently people who were crabbing at the time thought they saw a seal crossing a 4 mile stretch of water. Upon closer inspection, they realized it was a dog. After struggling to get him in their boat, (I guess Jim was determined to make it back himself) they took him the rest of the way back to port. I do not know if he would have made it on his own. Considering the time it would have taken to make such a swim, the tides could have changed, and he would have been driven back towards the islands. Again, I am not sure.

As well, there was a chance that Jim encountered a shark on this swim. Maxwell still remembers nights, immediately following the incident, when Jim would be dreaming kicking frantically as if in some distress. I can only guess that he was either simulating the motion of running or swimming, and/or trying to avoid a shark in the water.

I have heard it said that people impart themselves on others, including that of pets, if they are closely bonded. They will slowly and deliberately take on the characteristics of each other through time. Such was the case with Maxwell and Jim. I believe that the same love that acts as a glue to keep this world together also brought both of them back together. Jim ended up spending a long and fruitful 14 year tenure in this world. Though Jim has been gone now for some years, he will always be loved and he will never be forgotten. Maxwell will find him once again.

Chapter V

The Tao and the Clam

"All men will come to him who keeps to the one,
For there lie rest and happiness and peace.
Passersby may stop for music and good food,
But a description of the Tao
Seems without substance or flavor.
It cannot be seen, it cannot be heard,
And yet it cannot be exhausted."

(Reprinted from the Tao Te Ching, Lao Tsu, 1972, by Gia-fu Feng and Jane English)

It is hard to believe that less than 100 years ago we were still on horses. The car had barely been invented, the use of electricity was in its infancy, and long distance communication took place only through a single telegraphic wire. We say we are such an advanced society and yet time tells us that great advancements have only been made relatively recently.

Perhaps the next great advancement will be that of utilizing energy which is already in the body and redirecting it in ways that could literally change all that is around us. When you consider how little of our brains we actually use and how expansive our minds are, I believe this to be entirely possible. But again, if this is another great advancement it will take hundreds, perhaps thousands of years to play out. It is now not even readily understood or even known by the masses.

I do feel that some people at times, whether they know it or not, are using this same energy when they communicate. They are taping into an energy source that cannot be seen or heard, only felt. For example, when a person calls someone on the phone, only to find that the other person was at the same time proceeding to do the same thing.

I have a friend who lost someone in a car accident a number of years ago. She not only knew the exact time but also the exact place where the accident occurred, without having received any prior information. The energy perhaps that had flowed freely between these two people before the accident was suddenly gone or at least displaced. From what I know of physics and Newton's third law, this energy is never lost but only transformed from one state to another. The same law also speaks of entropy, whereby in the process of transformation some of this energy is broken down or degraded. The sun itself is considered to be nothing more than a dying star. The true paradox lies in with where this broken down energy goes. If matter is neither created nor destroyed, matter being comprised of some form of energy, where does all spent energy go. Perhaps this is a question that can only be answered when we die, if then.

People are nothing more than tightly bound bundles of electrical energy. All internal functions and external motions become electromechanical in nature. In addition, an electrical field seems to be generated that radiates outwards from our bodies. It basically envelopes us. When Maxwell sticks his hands into the water to clam, the electrical field surrounding him is attracted somehow to the electrical field generated by the clam. All life, including the clam, would have this same field. As well, water is an excellent conductor of electricity. It would serve as a pathway between two fields to theoretically help join them together. Electricity will follow the path of least resistance. Given this, is it any wonder that electricity has an affinity for itself. It has taken Maxwell many years of immersing his hands in the water to feel this energy. The pathway as well, can be easily broken through external distractions; i.e. Maxwell wondering where he left his boat or say a large jimmy crab taking hold of one of Maxwell's fingers. The energy cannot be seen or heard. It can only be felt. It simply takes focus and a stillness of the mind to sense it. It is known by many as the sixth sense of man. All of us have it, very few of us use it. If and when this heightened form of awareness is achieved, the work becomes easier and the number of clams caught greatly increases.

As mentioned, a clams movement for the most part is limited to up and down. A clam must be able to project itself downward very quickly in order to avoid predation and to protect itself from the elements. Those elements being storms, heat, cold, etc. This is a built in mechanism and part of a clam's survival strategy. It is as if a pocket is always present underneath a clam. Formed through time from the action of burrowing, it functions as a last chance retreat. When at ease or when feeding, a clam will stay at the top of this pocket. For feeding purposes it has to in order to maximize the amount of algae it ingests, perhaps even to eat anything at all. When Maxwell clams, pushing and pulling his hands through the bottom, he often can feel clams disappearing underneath, just in the nick of time, before his fingers have a chance to close around them. This tends to happen most of the time and it is a good thing. In this way, many clams are left in places that Maxwell has already worked. It is why Maxwell can work in the same place time and again. When Maxwell is not in focus, or at ill ease, it would seem that the clams are also not at ease and they will disappear long before Maxwell's hands even get there. Conversely, when he is in the right frame of mind they tend to not move at all. In fact being the social animals they are, if Maxwell is focusing with absolute clarity they have a tendency to move towards his hands. They also feel the energy being projected from Maxwell and are naturally attracted to it. Believe it or not, much like a good dowser finding water, Maxwell can find multitudes of clams this way. It is a physical action and yet is entirely dependent on the mind.

Like the Tao, a clam will reside in places that man rejects. The marsh is a place not readily accessible and difficult to move in once it is accessed. It is the very reason it remains unchanged. The clam goes about its work silently filtering out toxins from the water and providing nourishment for both creatures and man. In essence it will take something bad and make something good from it. And like the Tao it requires no thanks. In fact, both the Tao and the clam rely as much on the non-believer or people who will dismiss their value to give greater import to those that do. Perhaps to give any import at all.

Both the Tao and the clam abide in non-action. To take action would simply signify that something is wrong. In a clam action would mean retreating back into a protective shell until danger has passed. The interior of this shell imbued with the beautiful and soothing color of azure. How better for a clam to be consoled than by the color of its nacre.

Like a veil barely seen, the marsh will covert all that lies within her. On a smaller scale, a clam will covert all that lies within itself. To catch a clam is to catch a treasure. Over the years this became ingrained into the mindset of the clam hunter. The hunt became a pursuit of learning rather than that of strictly making money. A pursuit that at times came with considerable cost. And it would seem that nothing of any true value in this world was ever intended to be found easily.

EPILOGUE

2008

The days spent in pursuit of the clam, have for quite some time, come and gone. Though the passion still lingers, it seems with the passing of my friend Jim, came with it, the end to a chapter in my life. I still go clamming, but only when the weather is fair, and not as a sole means of income. As long as I have two legs to stand on, I will always frequent the marsh. I was in better shape back then and my back did not bother me as it does now.

I have resigned myself to a land based profession. Namely that of building houses. Though perhaps not as noble, the income is better.

It is doubtful that anyone will believe the recorded incidents in this book. It does not matter. I did not clam for either fame or fortune. If this is what I was looking for I would have chosen another profession.

If anyone should be acknowledged, it should be those people who continue to work commercially on small boats all year long. It is a dangerous profession. Especially on small boats. One would think that their lifeblood is the salt water. They remain undaunted, even with the prospect of securing better paying land jobs. The affinity they have for the water becomes apparent if one spends enough time working around them as I once did.

GLOSSARY OF TERMS

Stern transom	A cross member consisting of wood, metal, or fiberglass that serves as an attachment point for a motor on the back of a boat.
Lee	Referring to the side of a ship or body of land that is away from the wind.
Windward	Referring to the side of a ship or body of land that is toward the wind.
Danforth Anchor	A type of anchor consisting of two flat triangular plates with a long metal bar in the middle. The plates must grab hold of something or embed themselves into the bottom in order for the anchor to hold.
Open skiff	Referring to a small boat that has only a floor.
Rogue wave	Referring to an unusually large wave and often presents a serious hazard to mariners.
Predation	The act by which one organism preys upon another.
Symbiosis	Referring to the mutual cohabitation of two different species of organisms.

Pulling up to an area just off Sandy Point. Roughly two miles northwest of Wachapreague Inlet. The place to be worked is still about a mile away further up into the marsh. The only way to get there is by walking.

Leaving civilization behind

One of many small guts on the western side of Parramore Island. where clams and. oysters abound.

Driftwood. in the marsh indicating an area of slightly higher elevation where walking is possible. This particular windblown piece seemed. to serve as a perch for Bald. Eagles.

The number one tool of the Clam Hunter. His hands. Clams such as this can often be pulled from the edges of guts in large clumps. In mud they have a tendency to resemble large clusters of grapes.

A typical days catch

Digging clams and oysters on a small oyster bed in foul weather

Mud Dog Jim in his then familiar element

www.ingramcontent.com/pod-product-compliance
Lightning Source LLC
Chambersburg PA
CBHW020346290526
45785CB00005B/2175